THE SELF-CARE REVOLUTION

A GUIDE TO PRIORITIZING SELF-CARE AND IMPROVING MENTAL HEALTH

ALBERT HART

Table of Contents

INTRODUCTION

In a fast-paced world where demands and responsibilities often take precedence, "The Self-Care Revolution: A Guide to Prioritizing Self-Care and Improving Mental Health" serves as a beacon of hope and practical advice. This guidebook emphasizes the importance of self-care as a fundamental aspect of maintaining and improving mental health. By integrating self-care practices into daily routines, individuals can achieve a more balanced, fulfilling, and resilient life.

CHAPTER ONE

A. The Importance of Self-Care

Chapter one delves into the essence of self-care, highlighting its critical role in overall well-being. Self-care is more than just a trend; it is a necessary practice for sustaining physical, emotional, and mental health. This chapter explores various dimensions of self-care, including physical activities, nutrition, sleep, and relaxation techniques. It underscores that self-care is not selfish but rather an essential investment in one's health and productivity. By prioritizing self-care, individuals can reduce stress, prevent burnout, and enhance their capacity to cope with life's challenges.

CHAPTER TWO

B. Understanding Mental Health and Wellness

In Chapter Two, the focus shifts to understanding mental health and wellness. This chapter provides a comprehensive overview of mental health, discussing the continuum from mental well-being to mental illness. It explains common mental health conditions such as anxiety, depression, and stress-related disorders, demystifying them and reducing stigma. The chapter also introduces the concept of mental wellness, which encompasses emotional regulation, positive relationships, and a sense of purpose. Readers will learn about the interplay between mental health and self-care, and how intentional self-care practices can bolster mental wellness.

PART 1: FOUNDATIONS OF SELF-CARE

CHAPTER THREE

Identifying Your Values and Boundaries

Understanding and identifying your values and boundaries is the cornerstone of effective self-care. Chapter Three guides readers through a process of introspection to pinpoint what truly matters to them. By recognizing core values, individuals can align their actions and decisions with their authentic selves, fostering a sense of purpose and fulfillment. Setting and maintaining healthy boundaries is equally vital, as it protects one's mental and emotional well-being. This chapter offers practical strategies for establishing boundaries in personal and professional relationships, ensuring that self-care remains a priority even amidst external pressures.

CHAPTER FOUR

Building Self-Awareness and Mindfulness

Self-awareness and mindfulness are pivotal for understanding and nurturing oneself. Chapter Four explores techniques for cultivating self-awareness, such as journaling, reflection, and seeking feedback from trusted sources. By gaining insight into their thoughts, emotions, and behaviors, readers can make informed choices that enhance their well-being. Mindfulness practices, including meditation and mindful breathing, are introduced as tools to stay present and reduce stress. This chapter emphasizes the importance of being attuned to the present moment, which can lead to greater emotional regulation and overall mental clarity.

CHAPTER FIVE

Cultivating Healthy Habits and Routines

Establishing healthy habits and routines forms the bedrock of sustainable self-care. Chapter Five provides actionable advice on integrating beneficial practices into daily life, such as regular physical activity, balanced nutrition, and adequate sleep. The chapter highlights the significance of consistency and small, incremental changes, encouraging readers to set realistic goals and celebrate progress. By creating structured routines that incorporate self-care activities, individuals can enhance their physical health, boost their mood, and foster long-term resilience.

PART 2: EMOTIONAL SELF-CARE

CHAPTER SIX

A. Managing Stress and Anxiety

Emotional self-care begins with effectively managing stress and anxiety. Chapter Six delves into the various sources of stress and anxiety, from daily hassles to significant life events, and offers practical strategies for coping with these challenges. Techniques such as deep breathing exercises, progressive muscle relaxation, and mindfulness meditation are introduced as tools to calm the mind and reduce physiological stress responses. Additionally, the chapter explores the importance of identifying stress triggers and developing personalized stress management plans. By understanding and managing stress and anxiety, readers can improve their emotional well-being and enhance their overall quality of life.

CHAPTER SEVEN

B. Practicing Emotional Regulation and Resilience Chapter

Chapter Seven focuses on the essential skills of emotional regulation and resilience. Emotional regulation involves the ability to manage and respond to intense emotions in healthy ways. This chapter introduces techniques such as cognitive reappraisal, which helps individuals reframe negative thoughts, and the use of coping strategies like journaling and talking to supportive friends. Resilience, the capacity to recover from setbacks and adapt to change, is also emphasized. Through practices such as building a positive mindset, cultivating gratitude, and learning from challenges, readers can develop greater emotional strength and stability. This chapter empowers readers to navigate life's ups and downs with grace and confidence.

CHAPTER EIGHT

C. Building Healthy Relationships and Setting Boundaries

Healthy relationships are a cornerstone of emotional self-care, and Chapter Eight provides insights into nurturing these connections. The chapter discusses the characteristics of healthy relationships, such as mutual respect, effective communication, and emotional support. Readers are guided on how to foster these qualities in their relationships and how to recognize and address unhealthy dynamics. Setting boundaries is highlighted as a critical aspect of maintaining healthy relationships. The chapter offers practical advice on how to assertively communicate needs and limits, ensuring that relationships are balanced and respectful. By building healthy relationships and setting boundaries, readers can protect their emotional well-being and create a supportive social network.

PART 3: PHYSICAL SELF-CARE

CHAPTER NINE

A. Nourishing Your Body with Healthy Food and Exercise

Physical self-care begins with nourishing the body through a balanced diet and regular exercise. Chapter Nine emphasizes the importance of consuming nutrient-dense foods that provide essential vitamins, minerals, and energy. It highlights the benefits of incorporating a variety of whole foods, such as fruits, vegetables, lean proteins, and healthy fats, into daily meals. Readers will learn practical tips for meal planning, mindful eating, and making healthier food choices. Additionally, the chapter underscores the significance of physical activity for overall health. Whether through structured workouts, yoga, or simply walking, regular exercise is crucial for maintaining physical fitness, reducing stress, and enhancing mood. This chapter provides guidance on creating a sustainable exercise routine tailored to individual preferences and fitness levels, ensuring that physical activity becomes an enjoyable and integral part of daily life.

CHAPTER TEN

B. Prioritizing Sleep and Rest

Adequate sleep and rest are fundamental components of physical self-care. Chapter Ten explores the vital role that sleep plays in physical and mental health, including its impact on cognitive function, mood regulation, and immune system strength. Readers will discover strategies for improving sleep quality, such as establishing a consistent sleep schedule, creating a restful sleep environment, and practicing relaxation techniques before bedtime. The chapter also addresses the importance of rest and recovery, emphasizing the need to balance activity with periods of relaxation to prevent burnout and promote overall well-being. By prioritizing sleep and rest, individuals can enhance their energy levels, improve focus, and support their body's natural healing processes.

CHAPTER ELEVEN

C. Engaging in Activities that Bring Joy and Fulfillment

Engaging in activities that bring joy and fulfillment is a key aspect of physical self-care. Chapter Eleven encourages readers to identify and pursue hobbies and interests that foster a sense of happiness and satisfaction. Whether it's gardening, painting, dancing, or exploring the outdoors, engaging in pleasurable activities can significantly boost mental and emotional well-being. This chapter highlights the importance of making time for these activities, despite busy schedules, and offers tips for integrating them into daily life. By prioritizing joyful activities, individuals can cultivate a more balanced and enriched life, enhancing both physical and emotional health.

PART 4: SPIRITUAL SELF-CARE

CHAPTER TWELVE

A. Exploring Your Values and Beliefs

Spiritual self-care involves connecting with your inner values and beliefs. Chapter Twelve guides readers through a reflective journey to explore and define what they truly believe in and what principles guide their lives. This exploration can involve spiritual or religious practices, meditation, journaling, or spending time in nature. Understanding one's values and beliefs provides a foundation for making decisions that are in harmony with one's true self. This chapter encourages readers to engage in activities that nurture their spiritual growth, whether through community involvement, spiritual readings, or quiet contemplation, fostering a deeper sense of self-awareness and alignment with personal values.

CHAPTER THIRTEEN

B. Cultivating a Sense of Purpose and Meaning

A sense of purpose and meaning is integral to spiritual well-being. Chapter Thirteen delves into the ways individuals can cultivate a meaningful life, focusing on how purpose can be derived from various aspects of life such as work, relationships, hobbies, and personal growth. This chapter offers strategies for discovering and pursuing passions, setting meaningful goals, and making contributions that resonate on a personal and communal level. By aligning daily actions with a greater sense of purpose, readers can experience a more fulfilling and directed life. This chapter highlights the importance of regularly reflecting on and reassessing one's purpose to stay motivated and inspired.

CHAPTER FOURTEEN

C. Practicing Gratitude and Self-Compassion

Gratitude and self-compassion are powerful practices that enhance spiritual self-care. Chapter Fourteen introduces the practice of gratitude, emphasizing its ability to shift focus from what is lacking to what is abundant in life. Readers are encouraged to keep gratitude journals, engage in gratitude meditation, and express appreciation to others. The chapter also explores self-compassion, teaching readers how to treat themselves with kindness and understanding, especially during challenging times. Techniques such as positive self-talk, mindfulness, and recognizing shared human experiences are discussed. Practicing gratitude and self-compassion helps build a resilient and positive outlook, fostering inner peace and spiritual well-being.

CONCLUSION

CHAPTER FIFTEEN

A. Sustaining Your Self-Care Journey

The journey of self-care is ongoing and requires consistent effort and dedication. Chapter Fifteen focuses on sustaining this journey over the long term. It emphasizes the importance of regular self-assessment and adjusting self-care practices to fit changing needs and circumstances. Readers are encouraged to develop a flexible self-care routine that evolves with them. This chapter also highlights the significance of self-compassion in sustaining self-care, reminding readers that it's okay to have setbacks and that self-care is a lifelong commitment. By creating sustainable habits and remaining adaptable, individuals can ensure that self-care remains an integral part of their lives.

CHAPTER SIXTEEN

B. Overcoming Obstacles and Staying Motivated

Obstacles are inevitable, but they can be overcome with the right mindset and strategies. Chapter Sixteen provides practical advice for navigating challenges that may arise on the self-care journey. It discusses common barriers such as time constraints, guilt, and external pressures, offering solutions to address these issues. The chapter also emphasizes the importance of staying motivated by setting realistic goals, tracking progress, and celebrating small victories. Readers are encouraged to seek support from friends, family, or professional resources when needed. By developing resilience and maintaining motivation, individuals can overcome obstacles and continue to prioritize their well-being.

CHAPTER SEVENTEEN

C. Embracing Your Worthiness and Celebrating Your Successes

Recognizing and celebrating one's worthiness is a crucial component of self-care. Chapter Seventeen encourages readers to embrace their intrinsic value and acknowledge their efforts and achievements. This chapter discusses the importance of self-affirmation and positive self-talk in building self-esteem and confidence. Readers are guided on how to create rituals of celebration, whether through journaling, sharing successes with loved ones, or treating themselves to something special. By celebrating successes, no matter how small, individuals reinforce their commitment to self-care and nurture a positive self-image.

In the conclusion of "The Self-Care Revolution," readers are equipped with the knowledge and tools to sustain their self-care journey, overcome obstacles, and embrace their worthiness. By integrating these practices into their lives, they can achieve lasting well-being and fulfillment. This final section serves as a reminder that self-care is a continuous process of growth and self-discovery, and that every step taken towards better self-care is a victory worth celebrating.

www.ingramcontent.com/pod-product-compliance
Lightning Source LLC
Chambersburg PA
CBHW072343270726
48659CB00023B/2358